MW00562654

Year 'Round Fun

By Kevin Costley

Notes from the Composer

Year 'Round Fun is a three-book series of seasonal and playful piano pieces, beginning at the elementary level. Students from all backgrounds should find appealing pieces that relate to their individual lives. The pieces highlight the four seasons of the year, centering on activities, holidays, and events that occur in everyday life.

As with Book 1, Book 2 consists of pieces written in an intervallic style that encourages pattern recognition as well as creating excellent sight-reading opportunities for all students, including more advanced students. The pieces can be learned quickly and used for first recitals, festivals, and National Guild auditions. Above all, pieces in this series foster the student's imagination, celebrating the joy of life.

Year 'Round Fun, Book 2 is dedicated to veteran piano teacher, Karen Dolanc. I hope students and teachers enjoying playing through these pieces as much as I enjoyed writing them. Enjoy the "year 'round fun"!

Kevin Costley

Production: Frank J. Hackinson
Production Coordinators: Peggy Gallagher and Philip Groeber
Cover Design: Andi Whitmer
Editor: Edwin McLean
Engraving: Tempo Music Press, Inc.
Printer: Tempo Music Press, Inc.

THE FJH MUSIC COMPANY INC.

Frank J. Hackinson

ISBN-13: 978-1-56939-866-1

CONTENTS

Goin' to the Rodeo

Kevin Costley

The Big Wave

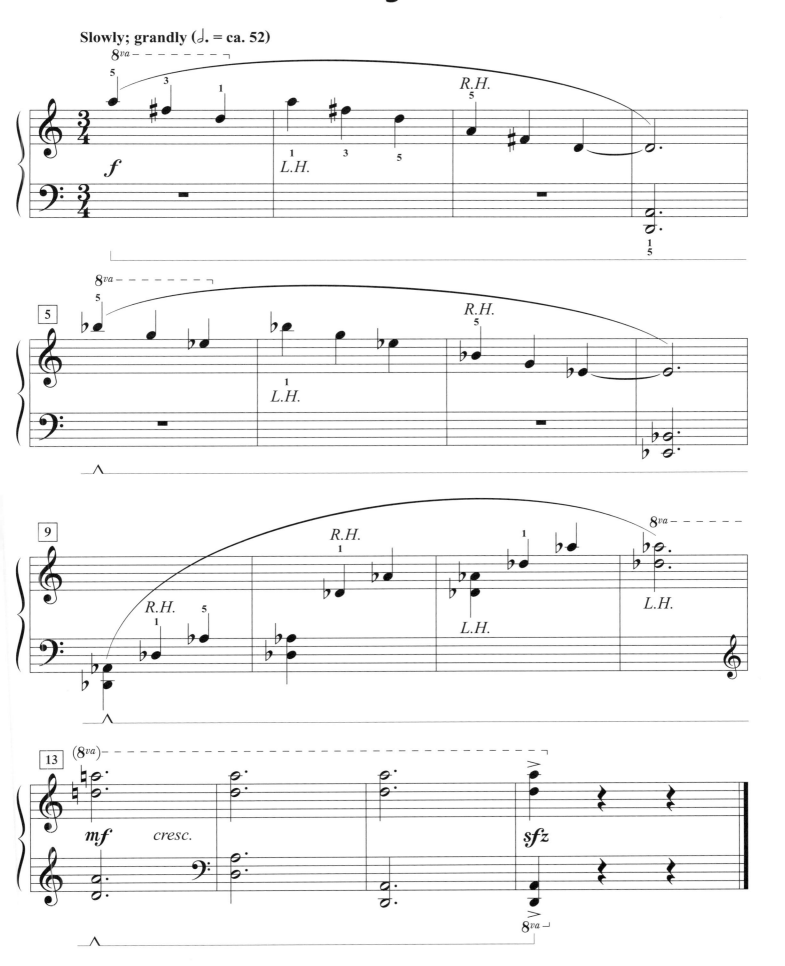

The Voyage of Columbus

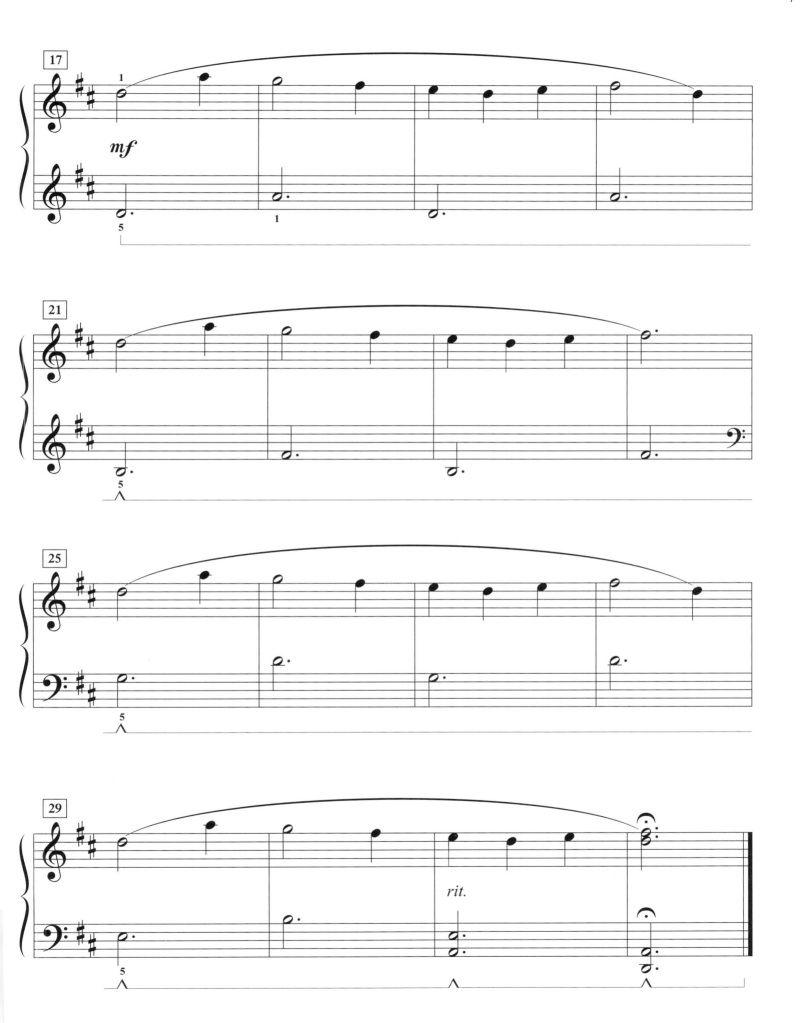

March Wind

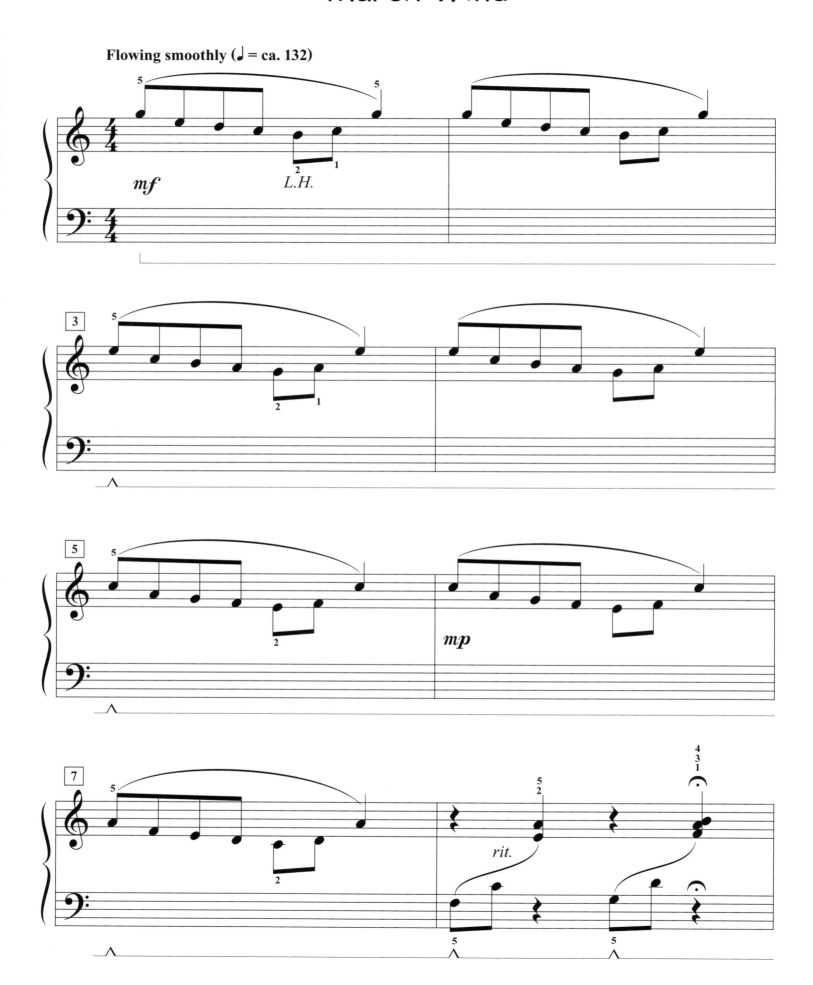

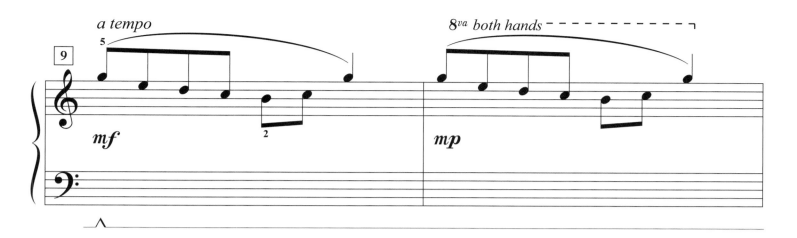

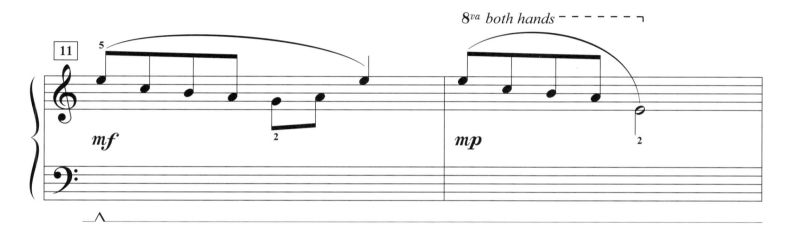

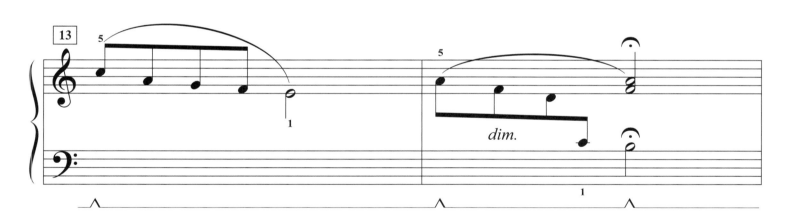

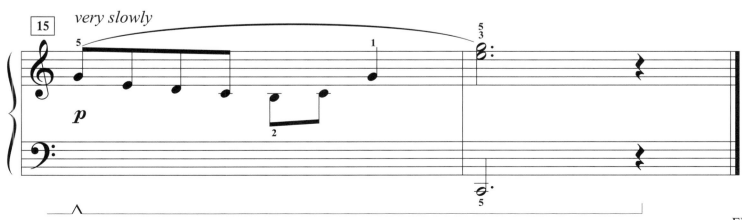

Ghost Hunt

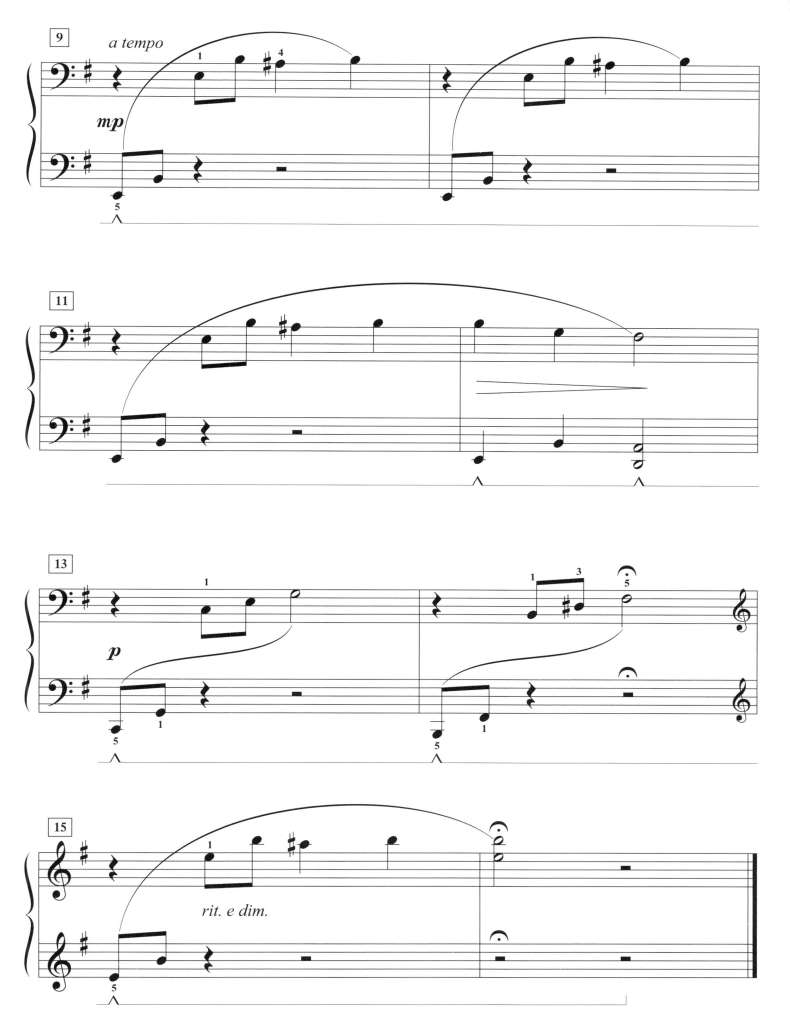

May Flowers

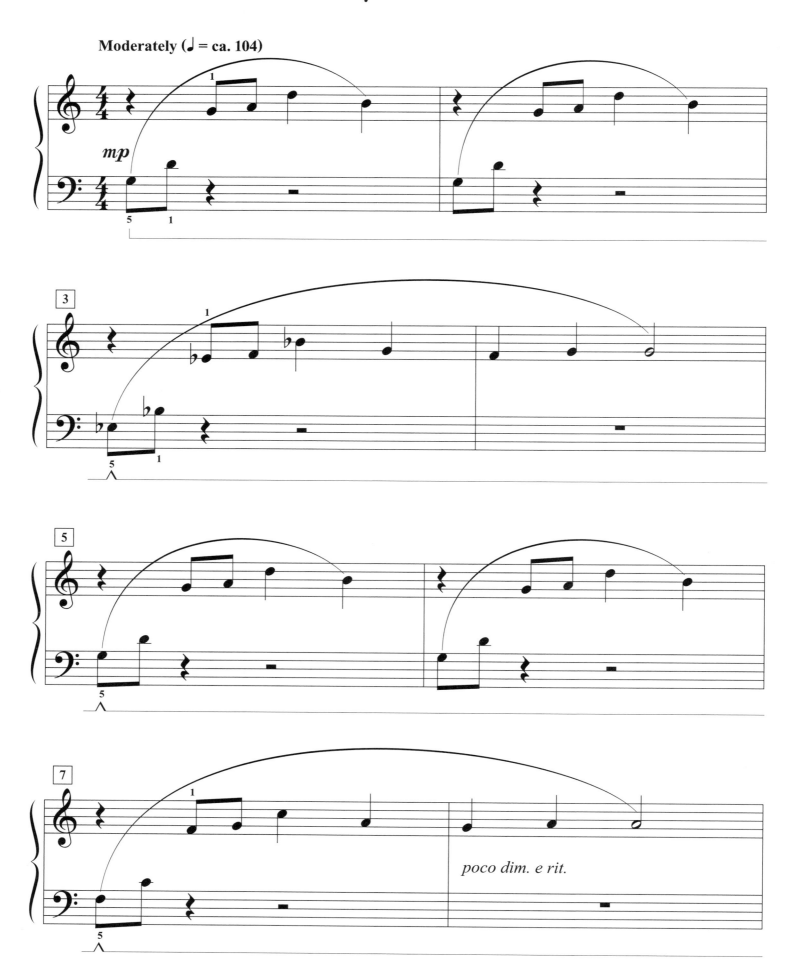

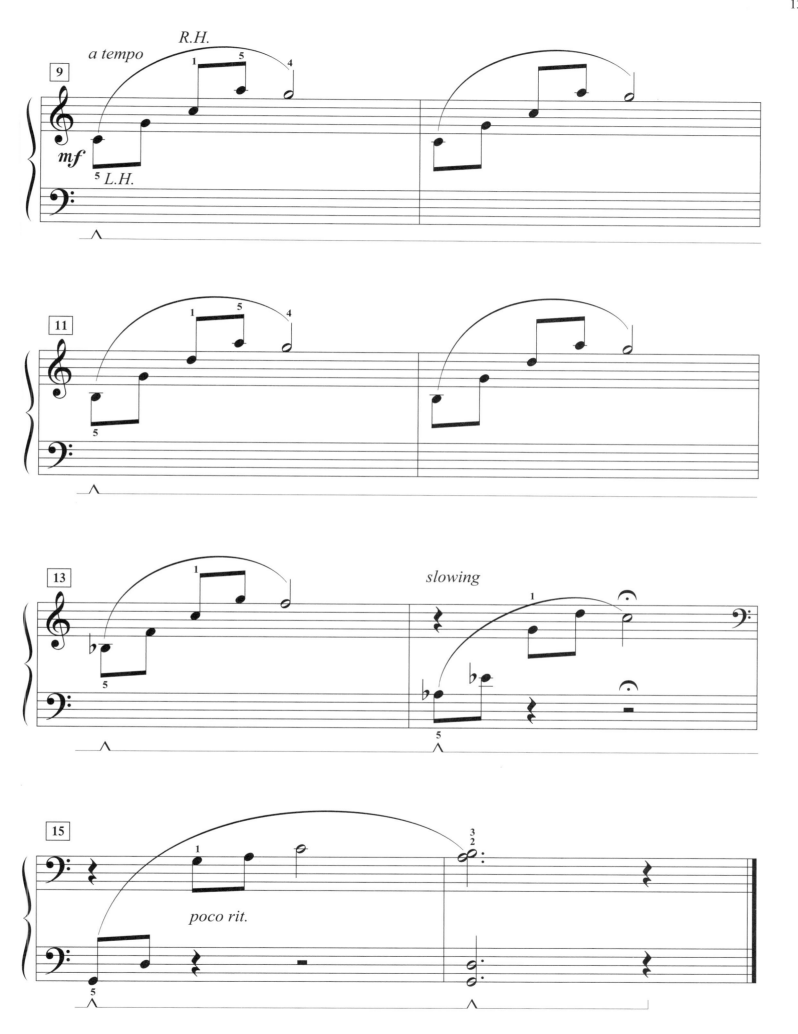

Hit the Beach

Chasing Butterflies

Summer Splash

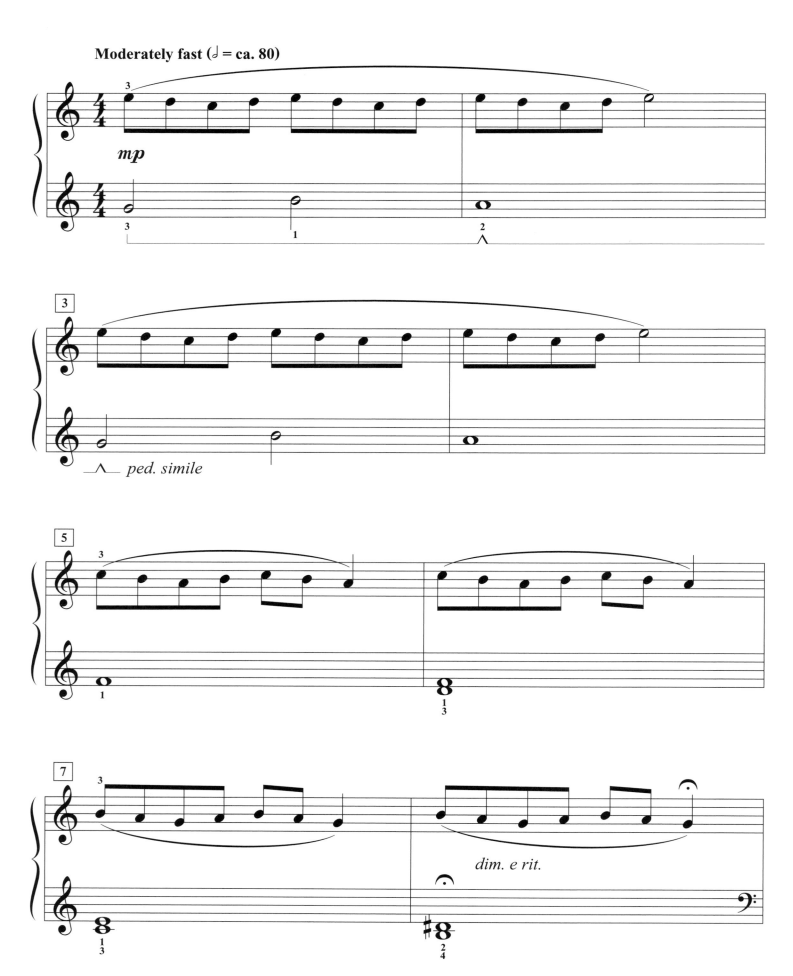

Snowflakes

Gone Fishin'

Sledding Down the Snowy Hill

Playfully (♩ = ca. 120)

April Showers

Penguin March

Briskly (♩ = ca. 132)

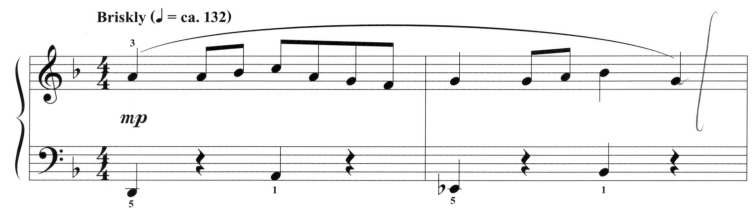

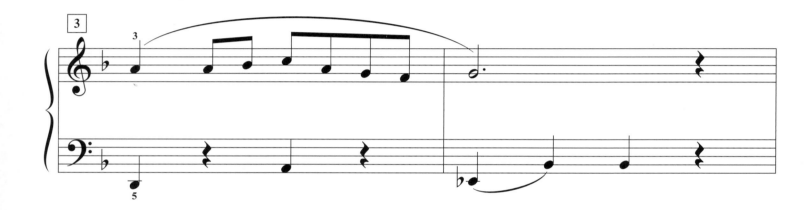

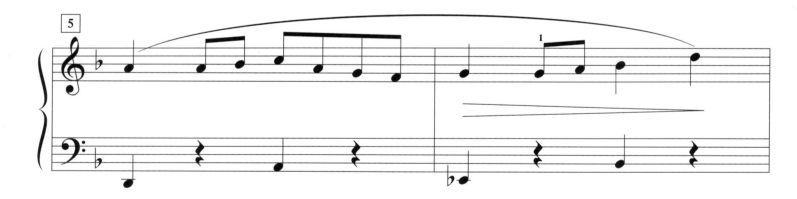

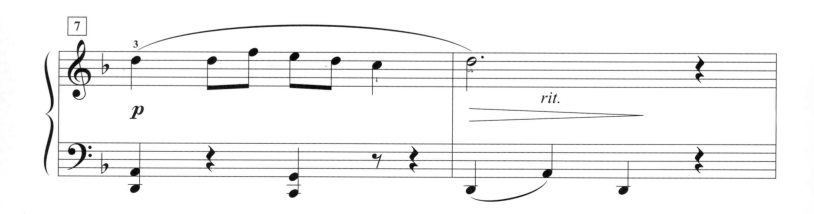

Johnny Appleseed